Say it With Words

Say it With Words

A collection of Poems

PA Timpani and Matt Post

iUniverse, Inc.
New York   Bloomington

Say it With Words
A collection of Poems

iUniverse books may be ordered through booksellers or by contacting:

iUniverse
1663 Liberty Drive
Bloomington, IN 47403
www.iuniverse.com
1-800-Authors (1-800-288-4677)

ISBN: 978-1-4401-2975-9 (sc)
ISBN: 978-1-4401-2976-6 (ebook)

Printed in the United States of America

iUniverse rev. date: 03/21/2009

I would like to dedicate this book to the following people: to my husband who through the chaos remains calm; to my children Jess, Matthew, Jeffrey, Michael, T, A, and N who have made me laugh and together we can make it through; to my Dad, who continues to watch over me, and knew someday I could make this dream come true; to my Mom who has always had faith; to my brothers, sisters, nephews and nieces who have kept me in their prayers and keep me smiling.

Contents

Matt's Poems

IT'S BEGUN

The beginning,

      Something new,

            To share together.

Hope is here..........

      Together

         Through it all

            It's about you and about me,

              Nervous?

               Excited?

                Laughter?

                  Tears?

    READY....?

      S ET........

         GO!!!!!!

               the journey begin

DO YOU REMEMBER?

A great thinking poem. One year for Christmas, my sister and I put together my parents' life stories. I included a poem "Do You Remember...", a history per se for the family. After all the memories, every stanza ended with: Do you remember...being there? The poem ended with:

Do you remember growing up?
Do you remember being scared?
Do you remember getting older?
Do you remember leaving home the first time?
Do you remember getting married?
Do you remember the birth of your children?
Do you remember your happiest times?
Do you remember your most difficult times?

Do you remember...
crying at the sad times?
laughing at the good times?

Do you remember the love of family always being there?

BECAUSE OF LOVE

You held me the day I was born,
Do you remember?
I don't
> Let me hold you,
> I can help you remember,
> when you can't.

Because of Love

You taught me how to feed myself
> Now let me make sure you are nourished.
You held my hand when I learned to walk,
> Now take my arm when we walk

Because of Love

You taught me to read,
> Now let me be your eyes.
You taught me how to drive
> Let me drive you, so you stay safe.
You taught me to make good decisions,
> Let me help you decide.

Because of Love

You taught me to take care of others.
> Let me take care of you,

It's because of Love

I KNOW IT HURTS

I know it hurts, but
I was there
when you heard the news.
I wanted to take away your pain.

I know it hurts, because
I saw you crying
and I tried to wipe away your tears
but I was crying too.

I know it still hurts now, but
you will smile again
And you will laugh again,
They will be in your thoughts
and they will stay in your heart.

I know it hurts, but
your pain will ease
and know that I will take care of your loved one
And I will take care of you
Until you meet again.

THIS LONG

I was there
    and I saw you
        in your last bed,
           sleeping.
Everyone saying their final goodbye.

Which is why
I can't believe
you've been gone
this long.

There is so much to tell you,
    to show you.
So much you have missed,
    but it seems like you've been here
        and at times like you never left.
But I feel you with us.
so I think you see it all.

I can't believe
you've been gone
    this long.

The family is changing every day.
    taking care of each other
But we're ok,
At times I can feel you
watching us

and I can hear your words
I think I see your smile,
But I miss your touch

I can't believe
you've been gone
            this long.

This long

IT'S A GIRL!!

PUSH!! PPPUUUUSSSSSHHHHH!!!!
It's a girl!!!!
A beautiful, perfect baby girl!!!

Oh, so pretty
in her dress of pinks or purples
laces, bows, curls and shiny shoes.

The dolls, hair and makeup...
        The c l o t h e s
phone calls, the giggles,
the tears, the arguments,
        the fears.

Growing to be a young lady,
in front of my own eyes
Opposite of me,
                like me.

The arguments put aside,
        advice now asked,
and laughs now shared.

It's a girl
        and now a beautiful young woman
My daughter.

SONS

The toys all over,
dirt on the face,
a mouse in their pocket,
sleeve is a towel,
clothes on the floor,
they're on their riding toys
girls are yucky.

But they have a smile
and say you're pretty.

Eat c o n s t a n t l y.
G R O W T H   S P U R T S.

Seasons are divided into sports,
baseball mitt here, hockey stick there
need to shave?
now they need money in the pocket,
a little more concern for the clothes,
they're driving now and
girls aren't so bad.

But they have a smile
and say you're pretty.

Eat c o n s t a n t l y.
G R O W T H S P U R T S.

Shouldn't they be done growing
no matter how tall,
they will always be my sons
to care about
to love.

ARE YOU OK?

I remember when I first held you in my arms
When I first touched you
When I first saw your face
And I looked at you
And spoke your name
I was worried that you were ok.

I remember the first time I took you to the doctors
And I was told it will be alright
I was worried that you were ok.

I remember the first time I left you
With someone to watch you
Did I tell them everything
I was worried that you were ok

I remember you going to school.
I was hoping you would have good days
And you would find some nice friends
I was worried that you were ok.

I remember the first time you went someplace
And I didn't stay with you.
I was worried that you were ok.

I look at you now, making decisions
You can still come to me
When you need someone to listen
And if you want, I can still give you advice
I will always be your Mom
And I will always worry that you are ok.

MY DAUGHTER

Over the years
I've watched my son
Grow
From a boy to a man

And one day
He introduces a girl to me,
He has fallen in love

And now this girl
Has become part of him,
By loving him,
Not by birth,
Part of our family
Like a sister,
Like a daughter
My daughter,

She is part of us,
I have watched my son
He introduces a girl to me,
He has fallen in love

YOU WERE, I WAS…

Did you know I always admired you

We had to share a room
And I tried to steal your clothes
But you were skinnier,
And you were always
The prettier one.

You were the neater one,
I was the messy one
You were the nicer one,
I was the loud one
You were the more helpful one,
I was always the brat
You were the more girly one
I was the tomboy

Did you know I wanted your advice

As we have grown older,
It no longer matters who is younger

Sisters
Through it all

Sometimes
You wish you didn't have one,
Until you talk to someone who never had one

WEDDING POEM

You took the wall down
You watched out for me
You taught me to smile
and how to laugh

You taught me to trust
and you taught me to love

For all of this
Only you
I want by my side
Only you
when I need to hide
Only you
in the morning light
Only you
can make things right

and Only you
I want to love

You gave me a shoulder to cry on
an encouraging word
a smile,
and a hand to hold

That's why I want
Only you
I want by my side

Only you
when I need to hide
Only you
in the morning light
Only you
can make things right

And Only You
I want to love

ON MY WAY

I thought
when I was young
I knew love
I was wrong.

I was on my way

Never alone,
but lonely.
Living my life,
but not feeling alive.
Missing the touch
of love.

I was on my way

Heard your name,
Remembered your smile,
Saw your face,
and we talked...
hesitated
and we dated...
scared.

and we fell in love

Wouldn't change a thing
on my way to you.

PRINCE MEETS PRINCESS

Once upon a time
        a little boy
                plays basketball
                        and has his friends,

        and a little girl
                picks daises.

And once upon a Time
        the lonely boy looks for girl

He sees the girl
        the first look
        the first smile
        the first word

And the little boy and the little girl
                grow to be a
        Handsome Prince
        and a Beautiful Princess

And once upon a Love
        Prince kisses Princess
and they live happily ever after.

YANKEES vs METS

Love is all about
>Differences
>>she's better, he's better
>Compromises
>>she likes, you dislike
>>he likes, you dislike
>Tolerations
>>she does, she doesn't
>>he does, he doesn't

And over the years
many thoughts begin with
>>I can't believe she....
>>I can't believe he...
and that's okay.

Only, and if only
the thought ends with
>that's who she is and I LOVE HER
>that's who he is and I LOVE HIM

ANNIVERSARY POEMS
(Since I wrote both, I can use the same lines)

AN ANNIVERSARY

Once upon a time
a girl met a boy
and fell in love

The story begins
The bride and groom
the exchanged rings
the lifetime promise
and their hopes and dreams

And so the story goes on
the ring is worn
the lifetime promise is kept
and the hopes and dreams have become real

Once upon a time
a girl met a boy
and they lived
happily ever after.

GOLDEN YEAR

My Dear Lord,
I wonder how can it be the Golden Year.
I look upon the years in wonderment
Wasn't it only yesterday
When I saw the eyes, the smile
That I fell in love with?

And I wonder how can it be the Golden Year
When I see the day, the church
And the ring sparkle
I can still hear our lifetime promise.

And I wonder how can it be the Golden Year
I still know our first home
I can still hear our newborn's cry
I am still watching our children grow
And now I am called 'grandparent'.

And I wonder how can it be the Golden Year
The one I fell in love with is still here
The laughter still makes me smile,
My ring is worn.
Our promises are kept,
And all our dreams became real.

To me, Lord, it is all Golden
For the years we have shared
Are as precious as gold.

BABY

It's a girl
It's a boy

I remember the first time,
nervously holding you
Looking at your perfect face
Counting your fingers, and your toes
Who does this baby look like?
What name do you like?

I remember watching you crawl,
Watching you taking your first step
The first time you said Dada, Mama
Your blanket

I remember your first day of school,
And awards,
And graduations

I remember your loves,
And your hurts
And finding each other...

And now your own baby
        And you will remember

BASED ON ECCLESIASTES 3:4

A parent-child version based on ' Ecclesiastes 3:4.
NO, I am not rewriting the Bible.

A time to teach, a time to learn
A time to love, a time to fight, and a time to love again
A time to talk, a time to listen
A time to take care, a time to be taken care of
A time to help, a time to be helped.
A time to laugh, a time to cry
A time to rejoice, a time for sorrow
A time to leave, a time to stay
A time for quiet, a time for noise.

BEAR

Give Bear a special place
So that you see his cute face.
Keep him near and when you're upset,
He'll be there for you to get.
He needs a spot that is just right,
Perhaps to sleep with you all night.
Bear will help you to know
That no matter how your day is to go
Know that I am just a call away
any time of the day......

I love you.

BEHIND EVERY PICTURE

Looking through the pictures
One of me expecting you,
The nurses cleaning you
Your first day home
You with your Grandparents
You on your Christening day,
with your Godparents,.

Behind every picture

Looking through the pictures
Your first smile
Your first step
Your first haircut
First day of school
Celebrations
Friends
Proms
Vacations
Graduation
Wedding Pictures

Behind every picture

Through the pictures
I see you growing before my eyes
and I have worried,
and I have hoped
and I have prayed
behind every picture

This is the quote that is on the front of the family photo album:

A wish
May you come together at day's end.
May you always have each other.
May you always have love,
And may God continue to guide you

BRIDGE

A bridge
      connected by love,
      to love,
      to each other.

A bridge to
the past to the future
the tears to the laughter
the hopes to the dreams
the quiet to the talks
the sorrows to the joys

A bridge
to meet
each other halfway,
for the two of us
to cross together

A bridge
      forever connecting us.

CRYING

I should be tired of crying
Dry my eyes
My eyes hurt

Wipe your tears
Does it ever stop

No,
Because if the tears stop
The feelings stop

And I never want to stop feeling
Tears for sad   Tears for joy

I never want to stop feeling

I'll cry a thousand tears
And a thousand more,
 But I never want to stop feeling

Wipe my tears,
        Dry my eyes
My eyes hurt
But don't let the feelings stop

DADDY'S DANCE

Look upon me
        your newly wedded daughter
As I dance with you,
        I feel the tears

My hope,
        he will love me as you have

We dance so slow,
        we are looking around
        both hoping this song never ends

Daddy, hold me tight
        You,
                I am so sure of
        hold me tight
            I love you

Don't cry.....
        to you,
            I am your little girl

I am so sure of you,
        hold me tight

Daddy,
        look upon me
            on all my days

DADDY'S LITTLE GIRL

He always thought of
Daddy's Little Girl

Dressing up
Dancing on his feet
Playing house
Playing with my dolls

And now a man asks Daddy
If he can marry this
Daddy's Little Girl,
This woman,

To wear a white gown,
To dance with for the rest of their life
To make a home together
To raise a family

This woman,
Now a wife,
Always Daddy's Little Girl.

DIVORCE

It was over,
before it ended.

She got the house and kids
He got the car
She got precious moments
He got his new life,
They played their own music

The wedding memories
were packed away
And the box was closed

He was leaving,
but he was already gone.

After ten years
He wanted to be single
She wanted to be loved

Wanted to be needed,
needed to be wanted

DON'T ASK

Don't ask me to wait for you
>> if I am here when you return
>> I may still be yours

Don't revolve your life around me
>> I may not be ready to be revolved around

Don't let me live and breath your life
>> live it the way you want
>> because there's so much to live for

Don't let me be a part of your life
>> if you don't know where you want me

All I am asking
>> if I am near,
>>> notice me

And if you want
>> you can move my heart
>>> by a kiss
>>>> or two

GOOD BYE

You didn't have
the words
but you
had to say
good bye.

But you couldn't
say the two words
you waited for me
to say them
and then blame me.

You wanted me
and I was yours
And then you
tell me
we can be friends
but you won't talk
and if you see me
you turn away.

And I'm not turning back
to see you
walk away—
I'm walking away.
You no longer want me.
I'll find someone
and we will say
hello.

I LOVE YOU MORE

I love you more
since the first I saw you
because you believed me.
I love you more
because you held my hand
I love you more
because you held me
I love you more
because you kissed me
I love you more
because you trusted me enough to make love with you
I love you more
because you asked me to marry you
I love you more
because you are a great Dad
I love you more
because when you should get mad, you don't.
I love you more
because you've stayed, when I thought you would leave.
I love you more
because you hold me at my saddest moments
I love you more
because you make me laugh
I love you more
because you accept every part of me
I love you more
because you touch me all night long

I love you more everyday
and if I don't always show it,
know it,
because I love you more now,
than I ever thought I could love you.

And my love for you grows more over time.

I REMEMBER

I remember the days
Rocking my baby to sleep
My baby climbing on my lap for comfort
A little hand reaching to mine
A kiss could make it all better

And I prayed.

I remember the days
When I 'knew' everything
Of teaching them
and of learning from them
Knowing all their friends
and always knowing where they were.
And I could protect them from the worst fears.

And I prayed.

I remember the days
when a red towel was a superman's cape
of watching them grow,
and of sleepless nights

And I prayed.

Now I have days,
of comforting the best I can,
knowing a kiss can't make it feel better.

And I pray.

Now I have days,
of giving advice, whether they want it or not.
Of teaching and learning
Worrying who they are with.
And knowing I can't still protect them.

And I pray

Now I have days
of tuxes and gowns
and remembering when they were little
and still sleepless nights,

And I pray

I remember the days
I prayed,
and now they are grown,
I pray.

IN MY MIND, I GUESS, I KNOW

In my mind
I can get out of bed
      without a thought, no problem
in these bones or muscles.

I guess, I know
My bones and muscles
are a lot slower
      …and ache.

In my mind,
my hair is still dark brown.

I guess, I know
My dark brown hair
has a gray hair
 or two
   or more
coming through
---natural highlights--
or angel sparkles?!

In my mind
I'm still in my twenties

I guess, I know
I can't be
The ones who call me "Ma"
and are now in their twenties.

(And to my mother's dismay
I still wear jeans and t-shirts.)

In my mind,
I can eat what I want
and it won't bother me.

I guess, I know
My breakfast,
comes a handful of pills,
  and with each doctor visit,
    there's less and less I can eat.

In my mind,
I still weigh what I did in high school.

I guess, I know
The rolls are there,
  I still have baby fat,
    just don't ask how old my baby is.

In my mind
My face doesn't have a wrinkle

I guess, I know
when I look in the mirror
I'm surprised to see who is looking back at me,
where did these wrinkles come from?

In my mind
I can stay up all night
  but now I'm just up more now during the night.

In my mind
In my mind

I guess, I know
My mind is playing with me
my mind is telling me one thing
my body tells me something else.

IN LOVE

I thought leaving was the right thing to do
I never knew we had it so good
Until you were gone

I've spent my life searching for what we had

And now I remember
I was happy, I was content
I was in love

I want to take you again
And not create what we had
But to remember
And to start anew
A love that never ends
Happy Content
I was so in love with you

LEAD ME

On the road to your home
You're so far away
I'm hoping you'll be there alone
The road beneath me
will lead me directly to your door

I know where I am going
I know who I am going to see
Just help me
I know where I am going
Lead me there

I need you
I love you
Let time be our friend
Give us time together

I know where I am going
I know who I am going to see
Just help me
I know where I am going
Lead me there

MAKE IT

As I sit looking around
in this lecture hall of sixty
I wonder how I am
ever going to make it.

I sat through fifty minute classes,
and now here I sit
(at least try to)
through three hour lecture

I am going to need help
to sit through this
and to get a 3.5
(or a 3.0 or a 2.5 or...)

MARIANNE

You let me tease you,
and you smiled.
You let me talk,
and you listened.
You let me complain,
and you advised.
You let me learn
and you taught.

You taught me
to do my best,
to be calm,
and to keep a smile.

Marianne, "Wanna Be"
(You wanted to be red.)
Red, the dictionary definition reads,
"being of or having a bright color'
Marianne, you made many of my days bright.
Bright with your smile and gentleness.

Marianne, "Wanna Be"
Because for you,
I want you to be happy,
To enjoy your new life,

To do your best to enjoy all days,
To be calm in the rough days,
And to keep your smile....

Know, that I will miss your smile,
And my wish for you:
May God continue to guide you,
And may you enjoy the rest of your "new" life.

Happy Retirement,

THE MUSIC PLAYS ON

I've always heard music
from the music boxes
to the radio
to the turntable
the music plays on.

Remembering my own
piano lessons,
Now I hear
 a piano- -
the white and black keys
touched by musician
that plays a hymn
for the parishioners
the music plays on.

I've always heard music
the music plays on.

This was to a inbound senior citizen my son, Jeffrey and I took care of.

MR. K,

I have learned from your words of wisdom,

Your acts of kindness have made my days brighter,

Your smiles warm my coldest days,

For this, you will always be in my heart.

MY FRIEND

My Friend,
Thank You.
In the quiet of my day,
when I let my mind wander
I think of those
I hold in my heart

My friend
Thank you

I think of you
For the friend you are,
For all that you do

Sometimes a laugh
or just the right word
You make my days brighter

My Friend,
Thank you
In the quiet of my day
When I let my mind wander
I think of those
I hold in my heart

THE MUSIC OF MY LIFE

As I sit here listening,
humming
the music of my life.

Remembering always,
My younger days,
with an old Protestant church hymn,
and where my beliefs could take me.

Remembering always,
the piano keys of recitals,
the strum of a guitar at a scout camp,
the beat of a drum on our kitchen table

As I sit here listening,
humming
the music of my life.

Remembering always
Oklahoma! Fiddler, and Anything Goes
(and many others)
on stage,
my child in the light.

Remembering always
my partner
with Frank Sinatra.

As I sit here listening,
humming
the music of my life.

May you always enjoy
the music of your life.

THROUGH MY MIND

Through My Mind
Humming through my mind, a song
brings me back to younger days,
when you could wish on Twinkle, Twinkle Little Star.

Remembering always
a song that hums through my mind
The music doesn't end.

Humming through my mind a song
is full of questions
as familiar as American Pie.

Humming through my mind a song
of darkness and isn't troubled by the Sounds of Silence.

Remembering always
a song that hums through my mind
The music doesn't end.

Humming through my mind a song
of young love and never wants to change
Just the Way You Are.

Humming through my mind a song
of watching a child grow from Sunrise, Sunset.

Humming through my mind a song
of a miracle in my arms to Rock a bye Baby.

Humming through my mind a song
of a promise now gone
and it's not just You and I.

Remembering always
a song that hums through my mind
The music doesn't end.

Humming through my mind a song
of struggling and hoping
When I'm Back on My Feet Again.

Humming through my mind a song
of a passing on, but life was My Way.

Remembering always
a song that hums through my mind
The music doesn't end.

Humming through my mind a song
of trusting and hoping that he's Somewhere Out There

Humming through my mind a song
of content and sitting in The Best Seat in the House

ORDINATION, 1981

Ordination…What is it?
according to the dictionary it says:
the act or ceremony of being ordained.
What does ordain mean?
to order, fix, decide, or appoint
It also means "officially appoint as a minister in
a Christian Church."

To be ordained, or appointed, is a big decision
Not only on your part, but on God's part,
the decision on His part—
whether or not to call upon Paul
or to call on someone else.
And, you heard His call and the decision was yours to
Go.

As God has been with you from the beginning of your time,
He will be with you throughout the time that lies ahead
He will help you to see light, when there's darkness
He will give truth when there are lies
He will show love when there's hatred
He will be there when there is death, instead of life
He will comfort you at times of loneliness
When you fail as well as you succeed, He will be
He will laugh when you need a smile
He will correct you when you're wrong
When you're weak, He will give you strength

Yes, God is good
The best to realize is God is there
He's there in every move that is made
every thought that is thought,
every heart that has loved,
every new path that is taken,
and yes, every ordination.
God is good and He is there.

Good luck
with the decisions that lie ahead
in the path that leads
and the unknown path that you have to walk
But God will be there, in every step

PERFECT

As bright as day, as dark as night
Will Love, can hate
Happy, Sad
Give anything, take everything
Tall, short temper
Sparkle Eyes, Crying eyes
Smart, stupid
Make you laugh, bring you to tears
Love you warm, leave you cold

The good, the bad
anyway
anyway you can

RETIRE

There was a yesterday
when I walked in,
and I was scared,
thinking only,
I will be here a bit.

The days
kept going forward
I made mistakes.
Not much more can I take,
and tomorrow I am going to walk out
but, oh, how I learned.
and I stayed.

The days
becoming years
going faster and faster
And sometimes thinking,
tomorrow I am going to walk out.
But with all the comings and goings.
and all the changes and challenges
I stayed

Now, the days are no longer waiting for
the tomorrow to walk out.
The day is today.

This is not goodbye
it is "I'll see you again,
another time,
and I'm glad I stayed."

But tomorrow
starts a whole new life
Tomorrow starts another journey,
with changes and challenges.
I had my yesterdays,
but I also have new tomorrows.

ROOM

9 by 12, 9 by 12
It's so small (oh hell)
It has a lot of things in here
A poster, my cat, and a teddy bear.
A window to look out and music to listen to
It's purple, didn't want blue

It's my room
When I need to be alone
It's just right for one
9 by 12, 9 by 12

It's so big
when I'm alone in my room

UNCLE

Dear God,
>   Thank you for the friends
>   that have become as close as family
>   that have shared my life with me
>   through good and bad, and the faith
>   we share in each other
>   and the faith we share in You

Hello, my friend,
>   I've been lately thinking
>   of all the years,
>   and all that we've shared.

It's been a long time
>   to grow and learn together.
And there are so many memories:
>   Bestman to Godparents to Grandparents,
>   Vacations to holidays to dinners.

And now we go on,
>   because the time has come
>   to take the new path
>   that Gad has chosen.

SYMPATHY

Through each of us,
Memories of your loved one,
Forever remembered

In my mind,
In my heart,
Their face
Forever pictured

Forever needed
Their love,
Forever felt

In my mind,
In my heart,
Their face
Forever pictured
Forever missing you.

THANK YOU

A great big thanks just for a great times. This is part of a poem written for a friend of the family. The stanzas between were filled with parts of our life together. He helped my sons learn to drive, and one line was "thanks for letting us drive your car (oops) and driving you crazy!"

There are certain times
I will remember all my life,
memories that I can't forget
Memories that I have,
never to be forgotten

Our time spent together,
a laugh,
a quiet talk,
time spent together.

When I think back on my life,
I will remember a time like this,
this is one of the moments.

These are the moments
that get me through
my life
when I sit in the quiet

How do I thank someone
for a day like today
A day forever in my memory

There are certain times
I will remember all my life,
memories that I can't forget
Memories that I have,
        never to be forgotten
              never to be forgotten

TIME

Once there was a time
Of love
And a time of hurtful words
And there was a time of goodbye

And time waited

And once there was a time
Of a glance across a room
And a time of a smile
And there was a time for a laugh

And time waited

And time wouldn't forget
The eyes that sparkle
The compassion
The words of love
The kiss

Time doesn't say goodbye
Time waits

SEVEN DAYS A WEEK

Seven Reasons to Love You
(although there's a lot more)

You don't care that I talk too much, or cry, or get mad

You listen to my singing and watch my dancing

Even though I'm freezing, you let me cuddle up to you.

You give me random kisses and hugs

You don't get mad when I'm late picking you (or can't pick you up)

You married me

You know that I am a giver, even though I take your covers.

STOP AND TURN

There have been changes
    (weight gain)
and loss
    (memory)
And I know sometimes I take too much
    (like the bedcovers)
I know there are times I over do
    (like on the charge card!)
and I know there are times I don't do enough
    (Like cooking, but that could be a good thing!)

But, with all the laughs we do share--
and, even with our disagreements,
I know I don't show
enough how much I love you.

And I love you.
Because you never stopped loving me,
and you never turned away,
I love you for not leaving,
I love for not yelling,
and taking all in stride.

You've been with me through the gains,
and the loss,
and the times I over do
and the times I do nothing.

Sometimes you feel put aside,
when I forget to show
how much I love you.

But , that's not how I want you to feel,
I have to stop,
and turn to you,
and not yell,
and just
LOVE YOU

TO BE ALONE

I need to be alone,
to be on my own.
I need to have help through my troubles
to have someone to listen.
I need to be wanted,
to be loved.
I need to be held
to be listened to .
I need someone to love me,
and for me to love them
I need someone to believe me,
to have faith in me.
I need someone to depend on,
to rely on, when I am down.
I need someone to laugh with,
to smile with.

Lord,
I need you.
to help me through my troubles when no one else cares,
to love me when no one else will,
to listen to me when no one else cares,
to have faith in me, when no one else believes,
to rely on when I can't rely on anyone else,
to smile with.

Lord,
I need you.
Is it too much?

YOU AND ME

Seeing no one
no one around
just you and me
listening,
talking,
walking,
dreaming,
won't change the moment
the best time is now
no one
no one around
just you and me
listening,
talking,
walking,
dreaming,
just you and me

MOTHER'S DAY POEMS

For Mothers' Day, I write a poem and make copies for the moms I know.

A mother's day poem,
>God gave Her
>Wisdom to guide,
>Eyes to see what she should,
>>and to know when to look away
>Tears, for joys and sorrows
>Voice to offer words of advice and comfort,
>>and silence.
>Heart to love
>Hands, for all she has to do,
>>and to hold.
>Strength to run towards or walk away.

>Mothers,
>for how they love,
>for all they do,
>for all they know,
>God gave us Her

MOTHER'S DAY PRAYER

Dear God,
Thank you for giving me your children in my care.

Thank you for my wisdom,
And for the guidance you give me
Thank you for the smiles they give me.

Thank you for giving me patience,
And for giving me strength
Thank you for the love they give me

Thank you for teaching me forgiveness,
So that in need, I can forgive them

And thank you for your angels placed around them.

And in this, I say,
AMEN

MOTHER'S DAY

Where do our 'job functions' stop? Could I ever put it on a resume? Never enough room! So, yeah, WOW!

MOM
>   the letters flipped upside down....WOW
>   and don't we always feel wowed?

>   A cook? A driver? A maid? An accountant?
>   A nurse? A teacher? A mediator? Seamstress?
>   Aren't we all this and more to our families?
>   We always feel wowed.

>   But I guess with a Thank you, or a smile,
>   or a hug, or an "I love you"
>   or when one of our own does something wonderful
>   We always feel wowed!

MOTHER'S DAY 2006 PRAYER

Dear Heavenly Father,

> You have put your trust in me,
> to give these children to me.
> And I am blessed to have them.
> I make mistakes, and you have forgiven me.
> And You know that I cannot
> get through a day without your help.
> Continue to guide
> and protect each of us.
> This I ask, in Your Name.
> Amen

GRADUATION 2002

HAVE A GRAND DAY

DREAM
For who YOU can be

BELIEVE
In yourself

Find HAPPINESS
In anything you do

Have PRIDE
In all YOU accomplish

SUCCEED
Not for others, but for YOU

LAUGH
Once a day

LIVE
to enjoy life

LOVE
someone

Have Faith in GOD

GRADUATION 2005

Your life is heading in a new direction
>No matter which way you go

>>Don't give up HOPE
>>>Do your BEST
>>Keep your SMILE
>>>Listen to your HEART
>>Make a LIFE, not just a living
>>>Have FAITH

>>May your new journey be happy.

GRADUATION 2007

The front of the card had a picture of a clock and a 'borrowed' quote about new beginnings.

The inside said:

Remember T I M E

>Think your plan out

>Ideas only work when you do

>Memories are yours to keep

>Enjoy whatever you do

AMERICA

**Americans, *

    ** Thank you,*

        ** For those who fought*

            **You gave us our freedoms*

        **The freedom of speech,*

          **The freedom of religion*

          ** The freedom to vote*

          **To hang a flag,*

          **The freedom to be who we are*

          **and who we are with.*

          **and where we live.*

*******We thank you*

        **For all you gave,*

          ** We remember you*

            ** We salute you*

TUESDAY

Are we United,
Each with its' own uniqueness
>> own quarter,
>> own flag
>> own license plate
>> tax variations
>> own landmarks
>> wonder of the world
>> or a sports team, or hall of fame

Yes we do Unite.
We come together in times of disaster,
We see it all the time.

And where were you on an ordinary day
A Tuesday, that started out as a typical day
Not a cloud in the sky
What were you doing?
You remember….

A plane.
>> a building,
>>>> and then again
this isn't an accident
>>>> and again
>>>>>> and again
This was much more than we ever could imagine happening.

What were you thinking?
Unspoken thoughts of fear on each of our minds.
What's going on?
Who is doing this to us?
 Are we next? Are we safe?
  We couldn't phantom why anyone could
 or would do this.

We wanted to be with our families
 making sure ours were safe.
We held our loved ones closer,
 because others never made it home.

America went on, we rebuilt,
 Fire fighters, police officers and airplanes don't look
  the same.
  Our freedoms are no longer taken for granted.

An ordinary day,
that changed us forever,
ended in an unordinary way.

We remember that Tuesday
There wasn't a cloud in the sky,
 but it was a dark day,
We held our loved ones closer to us
 their loved ones never made it home.

This Tuesday ended different, forever to affect us.

THANKFUL

This originally was an article I wrote in 1993. It was published in Western New York Family Magazine.

There are, oh, so many hectic days as
that I am not as thankful as I should be.
And with Thanksgiving approaching,
I've been doing some thinking.

We start our days at 5:30
-and to complicate matters,
we only have a one sink bathroom.

During the ride to work I start thinking and calm
myself down a bit.

I'm thankful I have a house,
I have food to feed my family
and that we have the necessities of life.
I'm thankful that,
some nights,
the kids settle for soup and sandwiches and say 'thank you'.

I'm thankful for their kisses goodbye and/or goodnight.
I'm thankful they say their goodnight prayers--even if
I'm not there.
I'm thankful for the smiles they give me.
I'm thankful that even when I'm at my worse,
I'm told "I love you, you're so pretty".

I'm thankful I have parents who care now
and cared enough to lecture me,
guide me and teach me along the way.

I'm thankful for my brothers and sister
for making me laugh and letting me relax when I go
'home'.
I'm grateful for the strength and support they've given me.

I'm thankful for my friends--the ones that help me out
in a moment's notice.

There are so many things that I am thankful for
            and sometimes just forget to sit down
            and relax enough to think about it.

Now there has to be a way to sit and tell myself and the
ones I love how thankful I am.

And I just thought of a way.......
            There are, oh, so many hectic days as

THANKSGIVING

As every holiday
      the time comes
that we gather with friends

We have so much to remember
      as the years go on

We have laughed,
We have cried,
We have comfort

Let us be thankful
      for the memories
And for the faith we share

Let us be thankful
      for the friends to be with

May memories,
      may friends
         may faith
      be with you in all the years to come

Thank you, God
      for these friends
      and moments to be remembered
      the faith we share
And the faith we share in you.

Amen.

CHRISTMAS, 1992

As I put the last tag on,
      and the last batch of cookies in,
      finish with the tree,
      sing a carole,
      mail the cards,
      and open more calendar doors.....

I realize
      Christmas
slowly crept upon us.

But I'm going home for
      Christmas
where the love of family is
For advice, a laugh, an ear to listen
and hearts who care

Another year
      slowly crept upon us
But I'm home
where the love of family is.

Merry Christmas
Happy New Year
and may 1993 be good to all of us.

Thank you for being you,
for all that the help you've given me
for the love we share
and for the strength you give me to go on.

Love, to all and may God continue to bless us.........

Christmas 2000 in lieu of cards, the family sent a poem.
Jeffrey wrote Christmas 2000, 2001 and 2002 poems,
and Matthew has continued the writing.

CHRISTMAS 2000

To Our Family and Friends

It's Christmas time all around
The snow comes to the ground
The happiness on people's faces,
Everybody is going places
The three kings and others with them
When Jesus was born in Bethlehem
Friends and family on Christmas Day
Jesus, in the manger he lay.
We all gather round the tree
Waiting for Christmas you see.
We gather with those who are near,
And wish the others could be here.
Merry Christmas to all
And to all a good night

May the peace and joy of Christmas
Be with you, throughout 2001

With love

CHRISTMAS 2001

The Three Wise Men
followed a Star to Bethlehem
to see Baby Jesus
and that's what started Christmas

The decorated tree
in the window for all to see.
Standing under the mistletoe
helps spirits grow.
People get a hug and kiss
by the ones they miss.
Families and friends celebrate Christmas together
And that's how it should be forever,
Listening to the songs of the season,
Everyone knows the real reason
With a wish, a thought
that cannot be bought
"That all hearts be true,
and Christmas Peace can be found in 2002"

The Three Wise Men
went to Bethlehem
to see Baby Jesus
And that's what started Christmas

Peace to all!!

CHRISTMAS 2002

To Our Family and Friends,

We seem to wait all through the year
and now the Time is here
The table is set for dinner
Out the window, snow shimmers
Lights sparkle on the trees
there are thoughts of those overseas
Children are having fun,
We light a candle one by one
We gather with those who are near
And keep others in our prayer

Houses decorated in silver and gold
Sitting around the fire where the story is told
of the very first Christmas long ago,

About The Three Kings and Jesus
May Peace be with us

A wish for you
May you always have health,
and love,
And may the true meaning of Christmas
be with you for 2003.

With love,

BELIEVE

I remember Christmas
Of long ago,
Looking through the catalogs
Waiting to go see Santa,
Sitting on his lap
And hoping he brings something I wanted

I remember trying to sleep Christmas Eve
And rushing down the stairs in the morn
And see the decorated tree
Piled with gifts underneath
And stockings stuffed by the fireplace

And then I remember the first year I didn't believe
The excitement just wasn't there.
I slept good on Christmas Eve,
But didn't rush down the stairs in the morn,
Open the gifts with my Thanks to everyone.

As my years went on, and I became Santa to my children,
How to get them to sleep,
"Santa won't come here if he knows you're still awake."
I would wake early Christmas morn, just to hear them
"Santa came, he really did!"

And then one time,
It was my turn to believe again,
Not in the man in the red suit,
But in what Santa means....
The surprise and the giving

And I will always believe in Santa no matter how old I am

CHRISTMAS PAST

Thank you for
        Christmas Past
and all that you do
        to make Christmas.

Now in the rush of going
from one store to the next,
I'm checking off the list in my head
And humming to the holiday music
(where's my next stop?)
I look forward to the relaxing moments of this season....
Sitting in Mass,
        a holiday concert,
                watching the lights on our tree
And I always remember Christmas Past

A Christmas Past
when I was little
A Christmas Past
going to look for Christmas trees,
school concerts,
Christmas eve with relatives
and old enough for Midnight Mass
A Christmas Past
baking cookies
A Christmas Past
at home
when the rush

was all taken care of
A Christmas Past
when Christmas Day
was home playing with toys,
trying on clothes
relaxing.

These Christmases
that I rush through
are my Children's
Christmas Past
and someday
they will have to rush through
their Christmas, as I rush through mine.

I know now
Christmas Past
was a gift of Love
from my Parents

Thank you
for all that you do
to make Christmas

MY WISH FOR YOU

I wish
for you more helloes,
 than goodbyes.
For you more smiles and laughter,
 than tears

I wish
for more loves,
 than hates.
For you more friends,
than enemies.
For you more good times,
than sad.

I wish
for you to be safe.
For you to know there is someone who loves you
I wish
for your dreams to come true,
And I wish
for you that at the end of your day,
You can say "Life is good."

I will treasure all of the memories
 and our friendship always.
Thanks, I would never have survived
        and I will carry you in my heart,
in my memory,
and in my laughter.

MATT'S POEMS

"Dedicated to the loving memories of
Herbie Pechuman and Ronald "King Ron" Butcher"

A LIFE LIVED FULL

my time has passed
and part of me is gone.
you were there to
help me through the hard times.
lying and waiting.
unable to do anything else.
less than two years ago
I planned a full Life.
as I lie down,
seeming like nothing bothers,
I realize these things for me.
a Life lived full is not to be
until death has come in the end to thee.
as I pass from my body
to die, is to complete Life,
whether it happens tomorrow or tonight.

AFTER THE TRAGEDY

What is your interpretation of this great nation
after the tragedy that shouldn't have had to be?
All those people dying without even knowing a reason
it's not even treason.
Are you going to be scared the next time you get on a plane?
Or will you decide to just take the train?
What if you're walking down the street
like you're going someplace to eat,
if all the sudden you see a Muslim,
are you going to start runnin'?
Don't disrespect others because of their race!
Although they have a different face
they are the same as you within
so don't put the blame on them.
So many people are scared
because they know this world has to be shared.
But if we all decide to cling together
then maybe somehow we can make it better.
It won't all be perfect
but at least you won't get shot by your brother
with a gun in his hand,
or won't have to bury your son with your own hand,
Those feelings hurt
even in the heart,
especially when you knew it could have been prevented
from the start.
So let's try to avoid this whole mess
and show each other a little bit of respect.

AT MY SIDE

before these crowded streets
I could always look at my side
and see you right next to me.

now I look around
to see everyone at their knees
yet I still only want you
and me to be.

keep your hand inside of mine
it holds me safe from this life
and when I see your smile
my shadows flash into the light
only as long as you are here
I shall not need
anything else so near.

BABY

Baby,
      Come and whisper in my ear
Tell me,
      Why you've been sheddin' those tears.
I wanna know
      Why he's not holding your hand
Come on girl,
      Where is your man?

Did he tell you that he loved you
And make it all go to waste
'Cuz I'm telling ya now
That you deserve brighter ways.

BRING THEM BACK TO US

bring them back to us-bring them back home
bring them back to us-like we never let them go
bring them back to us-bring them back home
bring them back to us-like they were your own

you make all the rules,
so that you're never wrong,
destroy the whole world,
if no one likes your thoughts,
do you believe,
we must always fight,
and never give this nation,
one peaceful night.
they forget their own lives,
to fight for a purpose,
of which they despise,
while their families worry.
war is only over,
when everyone is dead,
so there'll be fighting,
until our end.

bring them back to us-bring them back home
bring them back to us-like we never let them go
bring them back to us-bring them back home
bring them back to us-like they were your own

CHANCE

tear ourselves down not to be lifted back up
wear ourselves out not to be brought back in
lose ourselves in what you were
forever lost with these eyes blurred

one chance is all we want
one shot is what we never got

and that's all that we want
just one night, just one shot

I'm crawlin on my knees-beggin darling please
falling through the floor—can't take it anymore
was blind to misery—now it's all that I can see
when you're not here by me.

CLOSE YOUR EYES

took a step
          try to see what we were.
trying to find
          if we're just another boy and girl.
how do I know
          if this is more than just friends?
how do I know
          if you don't want this to end?

is it head over heals?
is this how you feel?

cloes your eyes – open your heart
tryin to find – what we truly are
let me know – let me see
what it is – you want us to be
just close your eyes

quiet and shy
          when it comes to my heart
can't seem to find
          what the right words are
just tell me
          tell me what you want to dream
tell me it's us
          it could be our reality

CUPID

the other day I wished
I wished that Cupid could help me out
now today I'm in bliss
so happy that Cupid could not come down

for if Cupid saw your eyes
he would fall as I have
fall far from the sky
and try to take your hand

DISAPPEAR

What did I do
all has fallen
this road is long
when you're walkin' it everyday
I'm still here
I'm still goin'
tryin' to find another way.

When the day is done-and the night is near
I feel this comfort-when I disappear
when my bleeding heart-has escaped to fear
to a place near you-i can disappear.

Find out where,
Truth shall lie.
With a chance,
With a chance that true love shall hide.
I will look,
I will see,
Finally find my destiny.

When the day is done-and the night is near
 I feel this comfort-when I disappear
when my bleeding heart-has escaped the fear
to a place near you-I can disappear.

DON'T WORRY   (dedicated to Not Telling)

don't worry
I promise not to make you fall in love
with me.
don't worry
we won't be the next best thing
then break.
don't worry
I won't start to gain your trust
then lie.
don't worry
we won't build up so high
then fall.
don't worry
I won't stay 'til it gets rough
then hide.
don't worry
you don't have to be scared
then freeze.
don't worry
I'll keep your deepest thoughts safe
with me.

DREAM

walk away
from this world now,
through the doors
that refuse to fall down.
all dreams of the mind,
you will become aware of.

walk on the horizon.
wash your face.
all of their dreams
become real in this place.
all kinds of expression from the mind.
works of all things with love and hate.

time is over.
pieces of their minds
I have now seen.
like mentors,
they show me their soul,
so I can now dream.

EVERYTHING WITHOUT ANYTHING

I wanted time
      and you gave me time
I wanted space
      and you gave me space
I wanted so much
it began to block my truth

With everything around
I could not see one thing
with everything I've found
I do not have anything

Anything without you
      is nothing to me
all my dreams about you
      are when you're with me
you could turn
      anything into everything
      with just your hand
make reality from these dreams
      when you're where I stand

FALLING INTO A BACKWARDS FLASH

resting down in my bed,
getting ready to rest beyond the end.
seventy-nine and twenty three days,
this is the age of my body to the earth.
only growing weaker like my father did just the same.
falling backwards to my father's funeral day
at the moment i see all of his friends walking up to me
many of them apologizing since my father's life
is something that can no longer physically be.
i arrive at the brunch held at his favorite restaurant.
the food is beautiful and my wife even better.
surely, this day of sadness shall never be forgot.
now leaving the meal to take a walk outside.
i realized i needed to inhale some fresh air,
since all of the memories are building up
that are at the moment to painful to bear.
instead of seeing the outside grass like i had planned,
before my eyes rest a newborn baby's hand.
it's my daughter for the first time that i see,
holding her in my arms i was always remembering
with that hand and a tiny grip,
she tries to clinch a hold of my one fingertip.
the beautiful eyes of my wife she has in her head,
like tiny marbles you would use to play with your friends.
handing her back to my wife,
i start to walk towards the room for men,
opening up the door to do my business,

i start to fall into that backward flash again.
instead of seeing that room i need,
i see a much better image of my wife and i on the beach.
another moment like the one with my daughter's hand,
my wife is snuggled up to me sitting in the sand.
our arms entangled so tight to each other,
as our fingers intertwine like vines in a yard,
never wanting to even begin to let go,
especially of this feeling that both of us now know.
look deep into the windows of our minds at one another,
we see everything that desires us to be together.
'stand up' i said as we get up to dance.
with the crashing waves as our orchestra,
and the setting sun sparkling down on us
as we realize a paradise only needs our love.
wanting this moment to last forever,
i only blink a second and fall into a backwards flash.
ending up before i met her and now on a stage,
only this image to receive my diploma on graduation day.
cloaked like a villain in a navy blue gown,
saying goodbye to many in my life who i'll miss,
a friend on each side with a wacky pose added along,
with the flash of the camera everyone else is gone.
fell again backwards into a flash where i didn't like to be.
my one friend in nineteen and i only three years less than he,
my thoughts going through my head.
everyone dies, but why so soon with him?
why was he chosen now to see the end?
too late to help try and help the cancerous liver.

very few hopes, but definitely not the same with tears.
the only hope i have is for his soul to heaven be delivered!
close my eyes and try to shed the tears,
falling into a backward flash to the start of my years.
see my parents and a man in a mask, gloves and coat.
i thought for sure it was finally my time to go,
but i guess all i thought was wrong that i was beginning
to know.
few minutes later i fell asleep and i'm so quiet,
until i wake up again in this bed of my body dying.
now i see the way it all goes in this journey of a lesson.
in the end, i saw the beginning and the rest of my past,
which all came from falling into a backwards flash.

FIND OUR WAY

My mind has been turning grey,
too mixed up and too far away
can you teach me again to see?
Maybe then I'll know what I believe.

When I'm rolling on in my life,
it seems as if I'm more wrong than right.
What happened to listening with your heart?
What happened to loving who we are?

Ever look up at the stars and wonder
if we were afloating there
would we be closer than now?
Did you ever think the only way
we'd be able to find a way home
is when they chose to fall on down?

FOREVER NEED

Our eyes may roam to find
but never will our hearts nor mind,
try to seek another or better
to this a journey that shall be never
i found in you a love that is true.
Another part of me in you
take my hand, into eternity we'll melt
a feeling with no other, my heart shall be felt
though may never always agree
it is still you I'll forever need.

GIVE YOU THANKS FOR LOVE

I give you thanks
for giving me your love.
I give you thanks
for giving me enough.
There is no way
for anyone to know
what you did.
When I you chose
a love built up in a life.
Can be taken away
gone so fast within a night
so I give you thanks
for sharing this love.

You have my heart
and you have my love.
You have my soul
and all my trust.
You have my life
and you have my death
and there is you and I
beyond the end.

GREY MIND

my mind always
black and white,
black and white.
can never go
colorblind.
I will always see
what I see,
different colors will appear.

my mind always
thinking the same way,
white and black,
white and black.
may not go colorblind,
though may go
lifeblind,
different visions will appear.

my mind always
white and black,
black and white.
colorblind, lifeblind.
can't trust all I see,
especially what I
see
all one picture coming in clear.

GOOD FRIEND

dear good friend,
I cannot seem to sleep
I'm afraid the thought of you
will be
when I wake just a dream.
how do I hold your heart
without a hand to hold?
float off to venus or mars,
maybe there I will know.
how you feel in this world.
if you would become my girl.

HELLO

Say hello
>   To the only time we meet
>   For the first time
Say goodbye
>   For no more we will see
>   Another first time
For everytime
>   Our minds continue to dream
>   It will be
A time after
>   Our first sight

HERE WE ARE

I know
we both love the way we are
so let's hold back
for just a small moment,
don't worry
I don't ever want to stop what we are.

I just need to see
what we have become together
because there was a time
I didn't believe
that you and I would ever be
now, here we are
in each others' arms.

It's nice to believe
that others look upon us both
and deep inside they wish
they had someone so close,
the way I have you now
I'm forever
and my heart's for you
it's a beauty in a mystery
Love has shown itself for just us two.

HOURGLASS MIND

Right now I hold you
      in different memories of my mind.
'cause I know I would lose you
      if I tried for you in the sands of time.
Walk all over options
      to find a way to your heart
All blocked and can't see the road signs
      so I ended up back in a dream.

I am falling down into the depths of my heart
crawling up the shaft that keeps us apart.

What goes on in my mind everyday
will never stop it's constant change.
Except the thoughts with you and I
eternally etched in stone for life.

I am falling down into the depths of my heart
crawling up the shaft that keeps us apart.

Caught within my mind
trapped with no escape
caught within my mind
and now it's far too late.

I AM ME

call me mysterious, or call me crazy,
call me lovely, or call me lazy.
it doesn't matter how you label me,
it will just peel off anyways.
call me up only to hear this voice,
or say my words are only noise.
this one will still be the same,
even if the peeled label has changed.

I am me, I am me.
no one else can I really be.
I am me, I am me.
my true self is what I wish you see.
because I am me, I am me.
no one else can I really be.
when I am me, I am me,
if somebody else, then I won't be free.

spread some rumors or spread some lies,
spread the butter when I dine.
but don't yell at me if no taste is real,
believe it's truth when I cook the meal.
change my name or change my style,
either way I'll walk my own mile.
words are poems until they are sung,
don't hate them what I have done.

I am me, I am me.

no one else can I really be.

I am me, I am me.

my true self is what I wish you see.

because I am me, I am me.

no one else can I really be.

when I am me, I am me.

if somebody else, then I won't be me.

I THINK

I think too much
I don't know what I'm thinking,
trying to find out what's inside
I hesitate,
I start to wait and draw a blank.
keep wandering.
nothing ever stays the same
on my mind
at the same time
I want it.
always getting
sidetracked
not knowing what I'm
thinking.
when I finally realize what's
inside,
it's always the same thing
but with a different
name.
always thinking about
one other else,
not myself.
I found some gravity
that keeps me focused
but I didn't know where it was going.
shown the whole world
I saw through somebody else's

eyes.
life is
complicated and
simple
at the same time,
it just depends on how hard
you are trying.

LET ME GO

from the inside of a bullet
it's so dark, I'm so blind
don't know where I'm goin'
gone so far, don't know why

you can only pull so far
before that trigger you hold
starts to reach my heart
walkin' on with the safety locked
too afraid to trust what you've got

just let me go
and let me fly
once you have gone
another I will find

LET'S RIDE

let yourself rain
down and rinse my soul,
reveal my mind to
a world unknown,
cleanse me clean
of all this meaning,
show me a real love
whose soul is beating,
I have seen enough
of hearts not breathing.

let's ride the night beyond the day.
play with life our own way.
we'll climb the steps to slide on down.
where we go we won't be found.

ride the night beyond the day.
play with life our own way.

LOOKED AT YOU

I looked at you,
you turned away.
I looked at you,
you darkened the day.
couldn't see me with those eyes.
couldn't give me any time.

I looked at you,
to see the world.
I looked at you,
beautiful girl.
couldn't see me with those eyes.
couldn't be the one you find.

I looked at you,
and saw your soul.
I looked at you,
we'll never know.
couldn't see me with those eyes,
love never born had just died.
couldn't see me with those eyes,
love never born, just a lie.

LOST PATH

when you feel like you're six feet below
where do you turn and where do you go?
thinking that all light has been shot out
and murdered by misery
who will bring you up from being down
who will help when you need to be found

trying all the ways that have worked out before
hoping inside they will work for you once more

LOVE

all efforts have faded
love turned into hatred
day changed into night
now I've lost my light

can't find the edge
when I'm in the dark
while I'm searching for you
deep inside my heart

love will make you live for today
love will make you show your ways
love will play tricks on you
love will make you so confused

it's bad when you are not
even worse when you think you are

LOVE ME BABY (OR LET ME GO)

Sittin around tryin not to think about you again
Makes me think of all the little things
The things we have and have not said
And if we keep rollin down this road
You and me are just gonna be
Two kids who'll never find their own

And all I gotta say
Is what you've gotta know
And that's love me baby
You gotta love me or let me go

Girl, if you ain't feelin this way
That I've been feelin lately
Then tell me so
And if you're gonna cut me loose
Then come on and do it soon
Cuz I'm tellin you now
You gotta love me baby,
Love me or let me go

LOVE NOTE

I tried—sitting down and writing to you
but the words,
like always,
they stayed within.
I tried,
liking someone else
but it's nothing like,
liking you.

You must be a real nice girl,
'cause now you've got two hearts inside of you.
you have yours to begin,
and now you've got mine too . . .

My heart is gone
and I know where to find it,
I don't want to get it back
take it as a love song.
they're my words I couldn't get through,
they're my feelings inside,
take it as a love note to you.

I haven't changed my ways
so I'm wondering
why does it feel like I'm living better days
you're my gravity
you keep me grounded
Signed by itself
My heart is a love note to you

LUCKY SEVEN

Seven numbers from you
seven numbers to dial
hear a voice whispering through
let's talk for a while.

Stay up all night
talk about the day,
what we like in life,
and what we want to change.

Call you up at night
on the telephone.
Only hoping inside,
that your voice won't go.

MIND

looking through the mirror,
past my eyes
and into my MIND,
walk down the hallways of
my memory,
open door,
only to find memories missed,
and memories more,
further walk on.
at what point do I stop?
keep proceeding,
a part of me I recognize.
how do I look to find what
I don't yet know?
where to put new information
when it leaks and looks for
a place to hide?
keep it building.
never expanding.
all in the MIND
that I saw
through my
eyes.

MY HEART IS CRYIN'

I felt a feeling I have never felt before
in my chest I felt a pain that's been hurtin more
so I decided to look around and find out
what it was all about

I looked and saw what I
thought I'd never see
inside I saw my heart
wasn't startin to bleed
instead it was . . .

cryin' out for you
inside
my heart is cryin' out for you
I might've had you off my mind
But I kept wondering why
I needed you so bad
When it's cryin out for you

Many times before I have felt this way
everytime I realized it was just the same
my mind, you were out of I thought
for good
but in my heart you stayed
and the strings you played
 to get it...

cryin' out for you
inside

my heart is cryin' out for you
I might've had you off my mind
but I kept wondering why
i needed you so bad
when it's cryin out for you

I'm starting to see
that I just need you by my side
to shed all these tears
that my heart would hide

MY LAST TWO CENTS

"Put in your two cents"
this is what I'm always told.
if you want to speak your mind,
you have to pay the toll.
What are we all coming to,
when nothing is without cost.
no more helping hands,
no more penny for our thoughts.
teaching us to manage money,
after every penny is spent.
how can we pay to learn,
we can't even pay the rent.
somebody with some sense,
somebody with a quarter,
please help us fill our wallets,
so we can have some order!

OLD ENOUGH

he calls her up on the telephone.
her sister is the one to pick up.
she speaks her words in a lecture.
on how she is not old enough.
old enough to talk.
old enough to listen.
old enough to love.
old enough to be with him.

ON MY WAY TO YOU

On my way to you,
I am finding that I don't need a map
my heart is my compass
our love will get me through.

On my way to you,
I've been up
I have been down
my feelings have been turning around
but they've stopped to stay
the same for you.

On my way to you,
out of all that I've seen
you are the only
for my heart to offer dreams
I went through life
On my way to you.

OUR INSIDE

The world could come crashing
down among us all.
when I'm with you
we're inside a place
that could never fall.
A place for no one else.
a place for just ourselves.
Every other out there
could wonder
wonder and start to stare.
But they'll never be inside
on the inside of this place
that's only yours and mine.

You pull me inside
a world that I,
never used to know.
You pull me inside,
a world that
only you and I could go.
And I would never step outside
of this inside,
of this inside with you.

Walk out these doors
is what I don't want to.
No need for
Jumping through any windows.

I could always use my two feet,
and walk another place else.
There's always a chance of that
something better could be felt.

You pull me inside
a world that I,
never used to know.
you pull me inside a
a world that,
only you and I could go.
And I would never step outside,
of this inside,
when I'm with you.

POSSIBILITY

Take a chance
and you'll see.
Look around and find all.
All of the possibilities.
It may not be too bad.
just open up and find out
who I really am,
And who I can possibly be
Do I feel like I probably should.
inside it's all confusing,
blinded and good.

Now you know.
you have begun to open the doors.
There's no reason to go
unless you don't want anymore.
What's out there,
that you can't find here.
Running around scared of your destiny,
when destiny is nothing to fear.

ROAM

going from place to place
        by every road I roll upon
it seems as if I can't get the thought out
        of every song becoming my home
finding comfort in not settling down
        since I can't settle down with you
write every song and play every note
        knowing when I'm done
        to myself I must stay true

SET ME FREE

Collapse to my knees as I tremble
all as if I'm kneeling to your soul
my arms fall to follow
as these hands I swallow

I try to search of a heart inside.
I try to find what belongs to you
When did you come in?
When did my love for you begin?

Take my hand for it will lift me up
I ask a chance to stand at your side
only a moment of you and me
For that moment, will set me free.

SHADOWS

Is this how it feels
when all that's around you
just can't take any more.
Is this what happens,
when you feel you're about to fly,
then crash right to the floor.

So much hope,
so many reasons.
kept telling yourself
it's all good luck,
finally on your side,
running back to get even.

Out of the shadows
your light is only to fade.
no longer to be seen,
no longer to show you the way.

SPEAK TO REVEAL

I lay my heart on the line
I say so much to you
my thoughts without compromise
now tell me why,
when I ask you this
that answer inside
you refuse to give.

So much I have heard before.
Calm down with your fear,
you can not hurt me too much more,
I will take what you give
even if you give despair
not much more can I fall
when my heart is at your call.

You tell me a tale with no end
without completion
our tale must stay pretend.
I cannot understand
why a frozen hand
if I you do not feel
please speak to conceal

With no answer
I cannot believe
it is I you do not see,
Please just end my curiosity
and speak what thoughts you breathe,
so that my heart
can travel on.

TELL A STORY

maybe my heart would believe
maybe then it wouldn't cry
if I told of you and me
waking beyond the sunrise

wake me in the morning when you're leaving
so I could kiss you goodbye
wanna know I wasn't just dreaming
your face in the morning light

tell me it's me
that you want to see
and I'll wait right here for you
say it's for me
that your heart beats
and I'll stay right here for you

only if I could tell a story
tell a tale with the two of us
maybe then in the morning
it'll be more
than a lonely heart's bluff

TELL HER

Look at you,
you crazy fool,
Don't deny the way you feel!
Time with her,
Your lost treasure,
when you found it made you heal.

Just tell yourself,
how she makes you melt,
In this paradise of a life.
don't turn this day,
just let it change,
from holding hands to holding hearts.

Anyone can say,
the way you've changed,
a new part of you is shown.
a brightened soul,
Some will never know,
once was lost and now you're home.

THANKS, FIREFIGHTER   (dedicated to Kenny)

When flames go up,
you are there.
You put your life on the line,
even if you are scared.

Scared of death
scared of lack of life
you put all this aside
when there is a fire to fight

All suited up in your jacket
Others just imagine what you might've seen
and without hesitation they are sadden,
You should be proud
especially for this
very Few could even go through it

Even if you are scared
you put your life on the line.
You are there,
when flames go up.

THE TALK

you said you wanted to take a moment
          so we could sit down and talk
so we're not walkin away with nothin' at all.
went on and on how I deserve better.
well maybe I do,
          but maybe I've already fallen for you

AFTER THE TALK

now as you stay up late
          on a lonely night
with the flicker of a movie as
          your only light
watching a romance comedy of
          what should've been us
laughing out loud about two fools in love
tell me is this a time
          that I cross your mind?

TO TELL HIM

I try to tell him
I try to get him to see
how to avoid a heartache
to prevent every misery.

Sometimes he don't listen
and other times he does
guess life is teaching me
how to show true love

It's when you're scared to fall,
          I'll hold on tight
in the darkest dark,
          I'll show the light
when you're all alone,
          I'll hold your hand.
but there's something you should understand,

Sometimes you hold on,
          and others you don't
The hardest part
          is knowing when to let go
at times you fall,
          and others you fly
but never let a dream pass on by

TOGETHER

Well I saw it in your eyes
when we lost all track of time
our hearts can never see
a place for us to be
together
       together
and though we may find
a chance or two pass by
it can never stay
always we must remain
friends forever
       forever
closer we shall grow
and more we shall know
a plan for destiny
we shall never be
together
       forever.

SILENCE

lay on down, time to rest.
don't you worry, this is not the end.
quiet skies fill this day.
those silent as in peace we pray.

and if your thought becomes a whisper,
silent eyes will be known.
for all will stop to listen,
to a life you once showed.

found peace in a life,
darkened days are shown the light.
final steps, why so long?
one you love, must now move on.

and if your thoughts become a whisper,
silent eyes will be known.
for all will stop to listen,
to a life you once showed.

UNDERSTAND

How do I tell you
that I'm going away
how do I tell you
that I'm not here to stay.

Don't get too close to me
pretending that it's me.
I have waited before
not waiting anymore.

I am here to leave
offer no sympathy
if I was here to stay
you wouldn't change your ways
so don't change now I'm gone.

Don't miss me now
'cause when I was around
you turned your back
it's not what I've become
that's made me the one
I'm not yours,
just understand.

VERY FAR

we can never get very far
if we only be what we are.
live for what you dare to dream,
die for the thoughts you really mean.
don't hold back on anything.
speak even when no one's listening.
do what you dare to do.
ignore the limits that
don't exist when no one's there for you.
must take a shot in order to see,
I'd rather fail than never be

WHY I WORRY

wanting.
needing.
it is you.
it is you.
to not tell,
is too scared.
the way I feel.
the way you might.
hoping.
wondering.
listening to what you say.
listening for the same.
worrying.
wanting.
how you feel.
how you might not.
this is why I worry.

WHY'S IT SUCH A SECRET?

why's it such a secret
everytime you find a different man?
and if I mean nothing to ya
why do you make sure I understand?

you know that I wanna
I wanna hold you with my heart
all I ask is a chance
to see what we really are

don't hold onto me baby
if you don't want me with you
don't keep makin me crazy
if so soon this won't be true
and if it's you I can not hold
just let me let you go
let me let you go

so why's it such a secret
everytime you find a different man
and when he decides to leave ya
you tell me like I'd never understand

WHO ARE YOU

Who are you
is what I want to know.
Where are you
can there I go?
Kiss your lips
as I hold your hand
See those eyes
as I barely stand.

Falling into
this way for us
Don't even know
what is love
It may be less
it may be more
All I know
it's better than before.

WINDOW CLEANING

There's an angel cleaning my window
I'm hoping he doesn't scrub too hard
I want there to be some angel dust left
Please just clear to rid the dark

There's another at my door
Looking all around to keep me safe
This angel is also cleaning
Making pure from the ceiling to the floor

Keep an angel on your window
The window will look as good as new
It will wipe all the bad away
So the light can shine right through

WISH

all of the walls closing in
just like the ones to her heart
can not see past the screen
no even to who we are
trapped in a world I can not explain
inside of this world I have not made

wish I could see how the blind man hears
wish it would help me escape every fear
a fear of not being afraid
when your fears are how you're made

broken movies in my mind
playing continuously through time
laid down to see a dream
instead I fell asleep

WITHIN MY ONLY HEART

I don't want you to get hurt
I don't want you to feel the worst
but if you ever do
I'll be right next to you

I don't want to see you cry
I don't want to see you hide
but if you ever do
I'll be right next to you

all the pain in life I can't keep away
all the shades of light will turn their grey
within my only heart
I swear I will try to keep you safe

you can't help but to feel the rain
you can't help but to know the pain
so when you do
I'll be there to get you through

you can't help but to know some fear
you can't help but to shed a tear
so when you do
I'll be there to get you through

all the days in night will turn to black
all the pain in life will make you unable to stand
within my only heart
I swear I will try to keep you safe

WITHOUT YOU

without you
it's twice as hard
to live with
my only heart
and without you
it's so hard to see
the daylight
from the misery

though I'm drowning without you
and keep on thinking about you
I'll try to forget about us
and sleep away the dream
cause if it's what you want
it's what has to be

WINGS

The wings we truly need
are always with us
when we believe.

Wings as a helping hand
wings as a joyous laugh
through the good and bad
Forever our angels
will always last.

May your
guardian angels wings
always surround you.

WHY DO WE CELEBRATE CHRISTMAS

All the traditions of Christmas
have been done before
The lights on the tree
Preparations galore.
Why do we do the same thing
the other years and this one more
With people in the streets
Waiting to meet and greet
some with bells
saying "and a Merry Christmas to You!"

This I will tell you
It's for the love,
and all that's deep inside
Surrounded by the people you're glad to know.

The holiday spirit in us all!
Light up your tree!
Sing a carole!
Enjoy a feast!
Just like the drummer boy knew
when he started drumming
Someone wonderful was coming
Family and friends,
their love is what we need
for the holiday spirit to grow

CHRISTMAS I KNOW

The snow is falling
But it just melts away
Silver bells ring
And I don't hear a sound
The tree is up,
Though no glow I can see
This Christmas feeling,
I can not seem to keep.

Old Kris Kringle
I swear he is real
Though not the same
To everyone of us

You're my Santa,
You keep this feeling here.
You seem to give
Me all this joy and cheer
With you, I'm shown,
A Christmas I can know.

There will be snow on the ground,
While the carolers sing
That feeling all around,
When silver bells ring
Red and green all over the city
Christmas angels looking oh so pretty

Looking through a crystal window
To see that tree inside
Watching how faces glitter and glow
Around Christmas time

THAT FEELING YOU CAN SEE

Sitting by the fire,
watching out the window
as the flames get higher
thoughts of mistletoe.

Like a child dreaming
of a city dressed in white,
at Christmas time feeling
Beauty in a sacred night.

With a song softly sung,
remember times of love,
in the melodies each year
remembering this simple cheer.

Tinsel all over the tree,
presents cover the ground
that feeling you can see
when the time of year is around.

LITTLE MIRACLES

Christmas is the looking glass
and when we look through the lens
we see what is to be
and what has always been

A million little miracles
right in front of our eyes
only to be noticed
around Christmas time

For it is a reminder
to everyone of us
to treat all the others
as if they were ones we loved

But those little miracles
if we look we can see
close your eyes and not your heart
just believe and they will be

Christmas is the looking glass
and when we look through the lens
believe in yourselves,
and the little miracles that have been

SHINE

When this time of year is coming so close
You try to find that feeling you have always known
Trying to believe why silver bells ring
Searching for the reason angels sing

When children are filled with joy as they pass on by
While the stars shine brighter as they hang high
Many dreams of your childhood you try to relive
You think they are memories only to be missed

Open up your heart inside
Sing a Christmas song tonight
Memories are not only to miss
When you let your inner child live

Help a stranger with their bags
Warm a friend's frozen hand
Let the warmth start inside
And let your Christmas spirit shine…..

COME

Come with me and stay
come for the holiday
come from outta town
come from not so far away.

Brush off the snow,
brush it off or let it sit
either way, come on over
be here in a quick.

Don't drive too fast,
don't drive to get lost
if there's a driving ban
just bundle up and walk.

See the snow fall,
catch a flake on your tongue
hear the carolers sing,
like when you were young.

Open the door,
don't worry about your feet
open it up with
a Merry Christmas to me!